MYSTIC MICHIGAN
Part Three
III

By Mark Jager

Revised
Volume Three
Fifth Edition

MYSTIC MICHIGAN
PART THREE
Revised

By Mark Jager

Published by
Zosma Publications
PO Box 24
Hersey, Michigan

All rights reserved. No part of this book may be reproduced or transmitted in any form or by any means, electronic or mechanical, including photocopying, recording or by any information storage and retrieval system without written permission from the author, except for the inclusion of brief quotations in a review.

Copyright 2007 by Mark A. Jager
Sixth Edition Revised Volume Three 2011

ISBN 0-9672464-1-5

Cover Photo
by Deana Jager
Copyright 2006

*Dedicated in loving memory
to Grandpa Petersen;
without him none of this
would have been possible.*

Contents

Gogamain Forest	7
Great Lakes Fish Calls	9
Singing Mouse	11
Passenger Pigeons	13
Earthquakes in Michigan	15
Michigan's Highest Points	17
Wonderland Snow Secrets	19
Secret Weather Omens	21
Michigan's Strange Glowing Fungus	23
Michigan's Cosmic Radio Station	25
Michigan Angel Encounter	27
Michigan's Buried City	29
Faces In The Falls	31
Michigan's Incredible Echo Chambers	32
Michigan Tree Tunnels	34
Michigan's Invisible Walls	35
Ghost towns in Michigan	37
The Lake Michigan Blob	39
Michigan's Nature Drums	41

Michigan's Primitive Rock Paintings	42
Michigan's Age Old Disc Factory	44
Michigan's Ancient Observatories	45
Michigan's Mystic Earth Rings	47
Michigan's Missing Race	49
Enchanted Forests of Michigan	51
Michigan's Healing Forests	52
Michigan Mazes	53
Michigan's Hypnotic Animals	54
Water Riddles of Michigan	55

Gogamain Forest

As long as storytelling has existed, tales have abounded of strange and mysterious creatures and people who lurk in the shadows.

There is a forest in Michigan that is gaining a reputation of being dark, sinister, and spooky. This incredible kingdom of darkness is called Gogamain Forest. It is located in the eastern end of the Upper Peninsula and is a part of the Lake Superior State Forest. It can be a land of howling wolves and hooting owls.

According to experts at the Michigan DNR, the forest is a cedar swamp that forms a canopy cover that is very thick and dense. Early in the evening, it gets amazingly dark very quickly. The shadows created by this forest are so thick that virtually nothing but moss grows on the forest floor.

The sheer darkness would seem to be a phenomenon on its own. There is, however, an even more awesome event that takes place in the woodland realms of Gogamain. The forest has an incredible temperature variation. Tom Rozich, of the Michigan DNR, commented on the forest's temperature. "The temperature differences inside and outside of Gogamain Forest can be tremendous. If it were a very hot summer's day with a temperature of 100 degrees Fahrenheit outside of Gogamain Forest, it could very easily be 30 to 35 degrees cooler inside the forest. In this forest it is much cooler inside the forest than it is outside of the forest in the summer. It is also much warmer inside the forest than out in the winter."

Great Lakes Fish Calls

Believe it or not, creatures from the Great Lakes may be calling out from the deep. Everyone knows that salt water fish such as dolphins or whales make audible sounds. However, it is not commonly known that there are freshwater fish that make audible sounds. Some of these types of fish lurk in the depths of Michigan's great fresh water seas.

Tom Rozich, of the Fisheries Division of the Michigan Department of Natural Resources, says that fish which were not previously known to make sound have recently been heard making noises. "I have a friend who was doing tagging studies on lake sturgeon down in the Lake St. Clair River. Divers were sent down prior to the time the fish were spawning. At that time the fish were calm and could even be touched. However, once spawning time started the situation changed. The fish began charging at the divers and were making strange grunting noises. As far as I know these grunting sounds were not known to exist up until that particular time."

The biggest lake sturgeon caught in the Great Lakes recorded by the Michigan Department of Natural

Resources was 310 pounds, 7 feet 11 inches. It was caught in Batchawana Bay on Lake Superior on June 29, 1922. It is likely that even bigger ones have been caught off record.

    Lake sturgeons are not the only type of fish that create strange underwater sounds. Other fish, such as the freshwater drum fish also make sounds. The freshwater drum fish makes a drumming sound. The drumming sound is made by the action of muscles connected to the swim bladder. The drumming sounds are heard more often during the summer and may be a component part of the spawning ritual. Perhaps early Native Americans were familiar with these drumming sounds and based some of their ceremonial drum beatings on them.

Singing Mouse

The motor city has produced a number of entertainers. One of the most sensational wasn't even human. It was a rodent.

Yes, it's true! Some mice cannot only squeak but are also reported to be able to sing. There are numerous stories of a mouse that could run up an octave while singing. This mouse inflated its throat like a bird, sang, and concluded with a trill.

According to English naturalist W.S. Berridge this singing mouse truly existed. On December 15, 1936, a mouse by the name of Minnie performed on a Detroit radio station. The listening audience heard what sounded similar to a canary or robin.

It remains an enigma as to when or how certain mice take up singing. Some researchers suggest that they are normal sounding rodents with inflamed respiratory organs. Another theory is that they are squeaking mice with very deep voices.

Some starlit night while you are out camping or hiking in the woodlands of the water, winter, wonderland, you may be entertained by a rodent. It is thought that a number of these strange singing mice exist.

Passenger Pigeons

Can you believe that there was once a species of bird in Michigan that was so numerous that each migration flock contained several million birds? Hunters killed so many passenger pigeons that they are now thought to be extinct, but are they?

According to reports, in September of 1929, Phillip Hadley, a U of M professor, was hunting in Michigan's Upper Peninsula when he saw a pigeon like bird with a pointed tail. His hunting companion, Mr. Foard, got a closer look at the bird and said it was a passenger pigeon. The eyewitness of Mr. Foard was thought to be reliable. The reason for this is that he had experience observing the bird in earlier years when they were still abundant.

Since that time, it has happened again. In March of 1965, a passenger pigeon was reported by Irene Liewellyn in Homer, Michigan. There may be many others who have seen the bird more recently. Take into consideration that even if someone has seen one recently, they probably wouldn't know what it is. Also, if someone did see it and happened to recognize it, how many would take the time to report it?

Earthquakes in Michigan

Did you know that there have been earthquakes in Michigan on many different occasions? Geological studies indicate that earth movement has been taking place in the Great Lakes region. However, the movement is taking place at such a slow rate that it has been felt only in the form of minor tremors.

According to records available at the Michigan Department of Natural resources, there have been 34 earthquakes in Michigan since 1872. The various epicenters are recorded from all over the state of Michigan, from the southern border to the Keweenaw Peninsula.

Historical writings indicate that Jesuits provided early earthquake reports. A Jesuit writing called "Jesuit Relations and Allied Documents" recorded the following about an earthquake in Michigan. "The savages were greatly surprised to see their bark plates collide with each other and water spill out of their kettles."

James Witherell, a judge in what is now Orchard Lake, wrote down the report of an earthquake by Michigan Indians. The earthquake in the following report took place on December 6, 1811. "The waters of the lake began to boil, bubble, foam and roll as though they had been in a large kettle over a hot fire, and in a few minuets up came great numbers of turtles that hurried to shore, upon which they (the Indians) had a great turtle feast."

The most powerful earthquakes that have ever taken place in Michigan were in the Upper Peninsula. One of them took place on July 26, 1905, near Calumet. The other occurred on May 26, 1906, south of Houghton. The earthquake in Calumet took place at 6:30 p.m. and is reported to have been felt throughout the entire Keweenaw Peninsula. It is said that a loud explosion was heard, and that chimneys were seen falling all over Calumet. Pewabic street south of Lake Lindon Avenue is reported to have suffered the worst damage. Nearly every chimney fell. One of the houses on the street was moved off its foundation.

The May 26 earthquake was the most powerful one ever felt in Michigan. Railroad lines were twisted and destroyed, and there was a notable sinking of the earth above the workings of the Atlantic Mine. The area that was affected by the earthquake consisted of 30 or 40 square miles. It is a geological fact that there is a possibility of earthquakes in Michigan in the future.

Michigan's Highest Points

In ancient times, primitive man viewed places of high elevation as sacred. Some of them may have even thought that such geographical locations were places people could go to be closer to God. This belief may be found in a number of stories from various religions.

If the primitive people of Michigan had such beliefs, they most likely would have traveled to the highest geographical locations in the state.

Michigan's highest point is at the peak of Mt. Avron in Baraga County. The elevation of Mt. Arvon is 1,978 feet, 9-3/4 inches. This peak is a very hard one to reach. In order to get to it, you have to drive down miles of rough trails. After this you have to hike a mile to reach the location.

The highest point in the Lower Peninsula is at Grove Hill, near Cadillac. Grove Hill' peak is 1,712 feet above sea level. At one time in Michigan's past a fire tower look-out station was located there. Today, all that is left to mark the location is the fire tower footings. There is not a panoramic view at Grove Hill, but it is a unique place to go if you have a desire to stand at the highest point in Lower Michigan.

Wonderland Snow Secrets

If you have a desire to enter into the treasures of the snow, you will have an excellent opportunity to do this in Michigan's winter months. In addition to the beauty and many recreational opportunities that Michigan snow provides, there are also hidden secrets spoken to those that want to take a closer look at these frigid natural wonders. Snowflakes accumulate in such abundance and blanket much of our state.

Ancient people believed that there were secrets contained within snowflakes. Some believed that snowflakes were microscopic patterns which contained mathematical and geometrical information about the unseen dimensions and other worlds. In fact, examining snowflakes through close-up photography reveals shapes that can easily be compared with many of the symbols used in the religions of ancient man. In addition, seven is considered by many to be a significant and divine number associated with the number of God. It is interesting to note that science has identified seven different families of snowflakes.

There is another bizarre phenomenon demonstrated by these tiny Michigan wonders. It is claimed by researchers that as you walk through the Michigan snow, you can identify the temperature by the sound it makes when you walk over and through it. A deep crunch in the snow as you walk means the temperature is only slightly below 32°F. At 23°F the pitch is said to rise and the snow creaks higher up the audible scale. At 5°F, the sound is reported to be unpleasantly high, almost similar to the highest notes on a violin being played badly.

Secret Weather Omens

Hidden in the forests of Michigan are living instruments that can help you predict the weather.

The earth has built-in weather forecasting systems that can be seen operating in a myriad of creatures in the timberlands of Michigan. There are so many ways of determining what the weather will be by looking at nature and knowing how to read its signals.

For example, bees seem to know when a thunderstorm is approaching. If you notice bees acting in an agitated way, it could mean that a storm is coming. Also, birds will gather together and sit on telephone or electric wires when they sense bad weather coming. Freshwater leeches can also be an indicator of changes in the weather as well. It is said that if you take a glass of water and put leeches in it, they will stay at the bottom of the glass when it is sunny and rise to the top when it is about to rain.

In other instances the link between animal behavior and the weather may have something to do with the humidity in the air. You can tell when a dry spell is coming because swallows and other birds fly higher than usual. This may be because dry air lifts flying insects higher, and swallows feed on flying insects.

There is one experiment you can do yourself that may show you what the temperature is. Step outside on a Michigan summer night and listen to the crickets. Count how many times it chirps within 15 seconds and then add 40 to that number. That number could be very close to what the actual temperature is, according to at least one source.

Michigan's Strange Glowing Fungus

Imagine walking through an historical logging area at night and witnessing strange and unfamiliar lights glowing amongst the brush and stumps where lumbermen once labored many years ago. Various Michiganders have reported seeing a bizarre fungus in Michigan woodlands which actually glows in the dark. However, one should not mistake this glowing phenomenon for the ghost of the old lumbermen. There is a logical explanation.

According to one eye-witness, the phenomenon of glowing fungus is found on pine stumps that remain from the logging era. "When we were children we used to go out into areas which has pine stumps left over from the logging days", said one Upper Peninsula store owner. "We would break open the stumps and the rotting wood could actually be seen glowing in the dark."

Joe Gates, a forest soil scientist who works for the US Forest Service explained the fungus. "There is a fungus in Michigan which grows on certain types of wood that is bioluminus. It glows somewhat similar to the glowing of a firefly."

Gates explained what type of wood the fungus is most likely to grow on. "This particular fungus seems to attack various groups of pine wood. I have seen this fungus a couple of different times. It is a pale green color. When you see it, it looks somewhat similar to what moonlight looks like when it shines on an object at night."

Your chances of seeing Michigan's glowing fungus are good. Forest Service officials report that the fungus is common in Michigan and has even been seen in pine tree sap.

Michigan's Cosmic Radio Station

What would you think if you were told that there is a cosmic radio station in Michigan that was designed to play music for alien beings from outer space? Well, this is no joke. There is actually such a station.

John Shepherd of Bellaire has $300,000 worth of equipment operating at his radio station; "Project Strat", which is designed to send music to the inhabitants of flying saucers as they whiz through our solar system.

Shepherd's station has 50,000 volts of transmitting power. He constructed the station specifically for aliens, and it can broadcast as far as 1,500,000 miles beyond the earth's ionosphere. As a cosmic disc jockey to the solar system, Shepherd sends out all kinds of music, everything from new age to rock.

Shepherd has converted a cabin into a radio station. He has built four high-voltage accelerators that are each 16 feet high. The rest of his cabin is full of various types of radio equipment. In his front yard stand two radio towers with the usual red blinking lights.

If you are interesting in hearing Michigan's cosmic radio station, you'll have to get your own flying saucer to hear it. The station broadcasts straight up in the air and is transmitted on an ultra-low frequency. As far as we know, he has yet to receive a message from aliens. However the station is in operation for 8 hours a day, 7 days a week. Shepherd is required to break for station identification by the FCC on a regular basis.

Michigan Angel Encounter

In recent years it is reported that there has been a number of people who think they have seen angels. However, people have been seeing them for centuries. A number of people in Michigan believe that they have witnessed this phenomenon.

Often the reports of this type of phenomenon come from people who are religious. In such cases it can be difficult to determine who actually observed something unusual or who was hoping to see something. In the case of someone hoping to see an angel, anything could become one to them within the confines of their own mind. However, when someone isn't looking for one and in fact doesn't even believe that they exist and then sees something, it seems more likely that something did happen.

Hubert Stoll of Cadillac was one such person. Mr. Stoll was not a religious person and he questioned the existence of God. Mr. Stoll witnessed something unusual long before it was common to hear of someone claiming to have seen a supernatural being.

One windy day in 1955, he was traveling down Hwy 42 between Lake City and Manton near central, Northern Michigan. While going around a sharp corner, he suddenly lost control of his car.

"My car seemed to go out of control by itself", Mr. Stoll said. "It went into the ditch and I was thrown out of the car. Looking into the air, I could see that the car was coming toward me and was going to land on me. That's when I saw bright white light pushing the car into the other direction so it wouldn't fall on me. The first thing I did was reach for my cigarettes. They were gone. I never did find them. Later, the sheriff arrived and gave me a ride home. He didn't even give me a ticket". Mr. Stoll said that even after all these years he still doesn't know what he saw on that stormy day in 1955. "It was and angel or something", he said.

Michigan's Buried City

In 1835 a lumbering town named Singapore sprang up in southern Michigan. Singapore was a thriving town with stores, sawmills and about 17 other businesses and buildings laid out on several streets. You can still visit many of the old lumbering towns in Michigan. Many of them have gone on to become good-sized cities. However, you won't be able to visit Singapore. Why? It is because it has literally vanished in time.

Singapore was located near Saugatuck, near Lake Michigan on the northernmost bend of the Kalamazoo River. Its population consisted of a number of lumbermen and people who owned the businesses to meet the lumbermens' needs. How did the town vanish?

After the Chicago fire took place, there was a high demand for lumber. Lumbermen at Singapore went on a wood-cutting rampage and cut down many of the trees within a 30-mile radius of the town. Once all the trees in the area were cut down there wasn't any work left for the workers. At that time, many of the people who lived there headed north to other areas to find work.

The mills were taken apart and moved to St. Ignace. Many of the houses were put on skids and moved to Saugatuck. However, several of the buildings remained. Singapore was located near sand dunes. The area gradually got covered by the drifting sands and by the 1920's the town was pretty much covered.

Some claim to have looked at old photographs that showed only roofs above the sand. A member of the Saugatuck Historical Society said that on of the chimneys from one of the houses could still be seen in the early 1990's. The chimney was covered shortly afterward. At this time, no traces remain of the once thriving lumber town of Singapore. It can only be found on the pages of history.

Faces In The Falls

For centuries people have sought the solitude of nature to find peace and tranquility. Waterfalls, springs and streams have always been considered special places because of the soothing effect they have. Various cultures believe that waterfalls and springs are sacred.

In the early 1990's a strange phenomenon occurred at a waterfall on private land in Munising, Michigan. The strange event happened while a photographer was taking pictures of the waterfall and its surroundings. The natural beauty of the area was breathtaking; however, when the photographer developed the photos he observed something even more amazing.

In the photograph, the water from the waterfall seemed to form what looked like an image of the face of an Indian. The picture was very clear. The timing that had to have been present for the photographer to take the photograph at the exact split second that the water was forming the image must have been against high odds.

The owners of the falls were happy to share their story but prefer to keep their names and their photograph private.

Michigan's Incredible Echo Chambers

The echo has been interesting to man since the beginning of time. Early man must have found it incredible to hear his own voice coming back to him when he yelled into a cave or out across a canyon. Perhaps there were some who mistook their own voice for the voice of a ghost calling back to them.

There are many places in Michigan where amazing echoes can be heard. However, there is at least one place that you can go in Michigan where you can hear an echo that can only be described as phenomenal.

At the far western end of Lake Mitchell, near Cadillac, there is a natural cove of water. There is a small rustic campground called Hemlock Park located at the back of the cove. If you go down to the boat launch on a crisp cold night when the water has a thin layer of ice on it, you can hear a phenomenal echo.

For the best results, you should go when it's very cold, still and about two or three o'clock in the morning. A regular echo is immediate. However, at Hemlock cove you can hear echoes that are estimated to be between three to five seconds longer or even longer. The echo will travel at such speed that you can literally listen to it traveling in a circular motion. If you shout into the cove your voice will literally move around the cove like a race care speeding around a circular track. The effect is similar to a giant outdoor stereo system.

Michigan Tree Tunnels

What are tree tunnels? Tree tunnels are formed when trees growing close together along both sides of a road, extend their branches and overlap at the center of the road forming a canopy overhead. This is not to be confused with a two-track. Tree tunnels form along several paved and well maintained roads in Michigan.

Although there are several roads in Michigan that qualify as tree tunnels, one has greater notoriety than the others. The tunnel of trees Between Harbor Springs and Cross Village on Hwy 119 is known as one of the longest and most beautiful in the state. It is a beautiful scenic drive through 15 miles of green passageway of varying degrees of thickness of the canopy.

There is also a beautiful tree tunnel located near Manistee. This is located on Main Street off of Hwy 55. This tree tunnel is about a mile or so long but it is quite unusual. The tree formations are unique and are an interesting sight to see if you happen to be in the area.

Michigan's Invisible Walls

There are places you can go in Michigan where you can experience extreme variation in the volume of sound. There are invisible "walls" you can walk through that will block out sound.

Most of these natural sound barriers are located along the west coast of Michigan. One excellent example of this phenomenon can be experienced on the shores of Lake Michigan along a place called Pyramid Point, near Glen Arbor Michigan.

At the bottom of a high cliff along Lake Michigan, you will hear the roar of the water from the lake. However, if you climb up the cliff and stand on the edge you will notice that there is an invisible wall that blocks out all sound. Once you go through this "wall" you will barely be able to hear any noise from the lake at all. The silence is so thick it's as if you can feel it. You will be able to stand there and look at the lake, but you won't be able to hear it. If you pop your head back through this wall and move a few feet, sound well re-emerge. The thickness of these invisible walls may vary according to where you are. Some walls may block out sound at a faster rate than others.

Ghost towns in Michigan

Some people think that most of the ghost towns in the United States are out west. This is not true. Actually, there are very few ghost towns out west compared to what there are in Michigan.

There are literally thousands of abandoned towns and locations in Michigan. Most of these towns were still striving in the late 1800's and the early 1900's. At that time there were hundreds of miles of railroad tracks in the Upper Peninsula that had towns built near them. There were also many iron, gold, silver and copper mines where towns sprung up.

There were once so many small towns in the Upper Peninsula that hundreds of them appear on maps from the late 1800's and early 1900's. At many of these ghost towns in the Upper Peninsula, abandoned stores and homes still stand.

One of the most interesting ghost towns to visit in Michigan is Fayette. Fayette is located on the Garden Peninsula in Delta County. In the late 1800's, it was a mining town that hosted the Jackson Iron Company. Nearly 500 people lived in Fayette. In the village was a store, an office building, superintendent's house, 40 log homes, a hotel, a machine shop, an opera house, 9 frame homes and barns. Part of the town looks almost like it did nearly 130 years ago. This is because part of it has been restored. There are no citizens in Fayette anymore. The public is welcome to visit the town and go through its' buildings.

The town even has its' own harbor, called Snail Shell Harbor because it is shaped like a snail shell. The harbor is surrounded by tall rock cliffs. As you walk through this 130 year old ghost town it's almost as if you can feel the presence of the people who once lived there, and hear their voices in the whispering wind.

Another notable ghost town in Michigan's Upper Peninsula is Pequaming. As of the 1990's it still had buildings standing. According to reports, Pequaming is 8 miles north of L'Anse. It is reported that water towers and large smokestacks from the town are still observable. There are many ghost towns that can be explored. If you are interested in finding one, call the county historical society in any of the Upper Peninsula counties you visit.

The Lake Michigan Blob

A strange and unusual blob appears in Lake Michigan in late winter or early spring that has many Michiganders mystified.

The bizarre blob surfaces for about a month each year and actually changes the color of the lake. Its color becomes a different shade of blue and actually looks like Caribbean water.

The blob is huge, hundreds of miles long, and covers the area all the way from Michigan City to Grand Haven. The Lake Michigan blob has actually been photographed by satellite. It is estimated that the blob carries more than one million tons of sediment. The setiment consists mostly of clay and silt.

On April 6, 1998, the Grand Rapids Press reported on the cause of the blob. It was written, "After the ice melts, the first big storm kicks sediment up into the water and causes the plume. The appearance of the lake's water subtly changes as clay and silt, not algae, come to dominate the reflection of light off of the lake. Algae typically absorb more light in the blue range than sediment does, so in sediment dominated water, viewers may perceive a turquoise blue color."

If you are ever traveling near the costal areas of Southern Michigan in the late winter or early spring, it may be worth your time to stop and see if you can observe the color change in the water.

Michigan's Nature Drums

There was once a legend in Michigan of mysterious drums which would be heard sounding in the distance just before a ship was about to sink. This legend is probably just a myth, however, unusual natural drums can often be heard along the shore of Grand Island, near Munising in Lake Superior.

Along the shores of Grand Island are huge and tall cliffs. At the bottom of these cliffs are small caverns or caves. As the waves of Lake Superior come crashing in, they hit these small caverns and produce a sound that is similar to the sound of someone banging on a kettle or bass drum.

The sounds are best heard in the still of the night. There are most likely many places that these drums can be heard. If you wish to hear these natural drums take a trip out to Grand Island. Look for a cliff area that has a small cavern in the bottom of it. At night you should be able to hear them.

Michigan's Primitive Rock Paintings

Ancient rock paintings made by primitive man can be found in Michigan. They are located in the Upper Peninsula near Burnt Bluff in Delta County, in section 24 of Fairlands Township on private property.

The rock paintings were first studied by W.B. Hinsdale, a famous Michigan archaeologist. Hinsdale declared the paintings to be authentic.

Some of the paintings are on the bottom of a 140 foot cliff. There are 13 paintings at the site. The biggest drawing is two feet, while the smallest is six inches. It is reported that pictographs can be seen from a boat along the shoreline when the water is high enough.

About 1,300 feet to the north of the first series of drawings are six more ancient masterpieces. There are an estimated 200 caves or caverns located near Burnt Bluff. Four paintings are found in or near Spider Cave, a 90 foot long cavern.

One of the paintings has been called "Big Man" by some of the archaeologists. "Big Man" is a two foot tall figure shaded red, painted in an ancient red dye. The figure's arms are in the air. The figure has a small head with a big body.

    Anthropologists believe that Spider Cave was once used as a place where primitive man shot arrows and threw spears. In nearby caves, skeletons have been found. More age-old paintings may be found in the future. It is thought that the paintings were made around 2000 B.C..

Michigan's Age Old Disc Factory

Believe it or not, Michigan may be the home of an ancient disc factory. Hundreds of circular shale discs were discovered near Alpena in the Thunder Bay area. Most of the discs were found by a father and son team, Gerald and Robert Haltiner. The discs are engraved with ancient symbols and the most common is that of the thunderbird. Thunderbirds were popular in the beliefs of ancient man.

Some primitive people believed that there were sea monsters in the Great Lakes that ate unsuspecting travelers. They revered the thunderbird as symbol of protection. Researchers tell us that people historically believed that thunderbirds sent down lightning bolts to kill sea monsters. Perhaps ancient man thought that if they had the circular discs they would serve as charms to protect them from the sea monsters.

Many other symbols were also found. Researchers believe that some of them were animals that were connected with the creation event. The discs are on display at the Jesse Besser Museum in Alpena.

Michigan's Ancient Observatories

Large ancient circular structures with walls that have moats dug around them have been found in several counties in Michigan. According to reports of archaeologists, the structures are between 1,500 and 5,000 years old. It hasn't been proven at this time; however, there are some researchers who believe that these circular earthen structures may have been used as calendars to mark the movement of the zodiac.

A large circle of stones, 397 feet in circumference was investigated in the early 1990's on Beaver Island. Experts determined that the structure probably served as a calendar for migrating fishermen thousands of years ago. But the most incredible discovery of all has taken place in recent years on the northeastern side of the state near Alpena. Stone formations have been found that some researchers believe is an ancient calendar of the zodiac that is acres big!

Stone walls made of rock that run for hundreds of feet, then veer of at right angles are visible at the site. Within the confines of the walls are stone piles or cairns. What is a cairn? A cairn is a boundary stone which serves as a marker or guide. It is a mound of stones that serve as a burial cover or as a sighting point for an ancient calendar. The cairns in the walled structure near Alpena are conical in shape. A person can climb down into the center of these conical cairns and remain upright. Some of the cairns are 12 feet across and 5 feet high. Similar rock piles and cairns are reported to have been found in Thunder Bay, Canada by Greg Bambeneck and Glen Langhorst, who are anthropologists from Duluth Minnesota.

    The piles are thought by some to be part of an ancient observatory, although this belief is debatable. No one can prove who made the various structures across the state. The fact that people from Michigan who once lived here may have built them is thought provoking. The acres big oddity is located at South Pointe near the Black River which is south of Alpena and north of Harrisville.

Michigan's Mystic Earth Rings

Ancient Michiganders with an odd culture built large circular, earthen structures in various places with-in the state. There are four of them found with-in a mile and a half of Selkirk in sections 33 and 34 of west Branch Township.

The largest ring is 300 feet east and west, of 280 feet north and south. One of the other circular earthen constructions is made like a huge compass. It has 8 openings in it. The openings mark each cardinal and intermediate compass point. One of the earthworks is not circular but is rectangular. The rectangular structure is reported to have an opening in it that is about 206 feet. The construction is said to be made of about 400 feet of soil.

The incredible earthworks are thought to be anywhere between 1,500 and 5,000 years old, according to some scholars. Some archaeologists believe that those who built them worshipped the sun. There are different theories as to what they were used for. Some believe they were forts, others believe they were ancient calendars marking the movement of the planets and signs of the zodiac. Others theorize that they were magical circles used in shamanistic ceremonies. Some researchers think that there were once roofs on these structures and that they were used as temples.

A few of these primitive constructions are still well preserved. The circular and rectangular structures are composed of dirt rather than rock like the Beaver Island structure. There are various hypotheses on them. The biggest question concerning the age old formations is; who built them?

Michigan's Missing Race

There is evidence that can be found all over Michigan that indicates that some type of advanced civilization lived in the state at one time.

A large stone henge type structure has been found on Beaver Island. Large circular earthwork rings have been found in Missaukee and other counties. Earthen pyramids have been studied near Ontonogon. Ancient copper mines have been explored on the Keeweenaw Peninsula. A long rock wall which encases cairns has been studied near Alpena. Some of these structures are thought to date back to about 2000 B.C. or earlier. It appears as if the culture that built them may have pre-dated the early Indian tribes.

Some scientists now believe that the old theory of plate tectonics may be wrong. The new plate tectonic theory called catastrophic plate tectonics states that the continents did not split apart slowly over periods of thousands of years, but rather split apart very rapidly during a world-wide catastrophic flood.

Scientists state that before the continents split there was a super continent called Pangea. Geologists believe that before the continents split, Michigan was in the north central portion of this continent.

If you imagine the continents placed back together you will notice that the latitudes of the stone hedge type formation on Beaver Island and the ancient earthwork rings of Northern Michigan are somewhat on the same latitude as stone hedge in England.

According to Biblical scholars, the great flood took place about 4,000 years ago around 2,000 B.C.. There is a possibility that some of the ancient structures that have been found in Michigan may be remnants from a long forgotten culture that perished in the days of Noah and the Biblical flood.

This would explain how this ancient Michigan culture vanished. Stone or copper tablets with hieroglyphics have been discovered in Michigan that depict a universal flood. The very ground beneath your feet may have been tread upon by the citizens of an age old civilization. The people of God will one day walk on the remnants of this civilization. Will you walk in the footsteps of those that were destroyed, or follow the example of Noah?

Enchanted Forests of Michigan

Northern Michigan's autumns are some of the most beautiful in the world. The timbers in the great northern cathedral break forth into psychedelic colors, and almost seem to sing.

The trees in the woodland shrines have been here for a long time. In fact, there are some trees that are thought to have been standing for nearly 400 years or more.

There can be quite a large number of trees per acre in Michigan. For example, in a mature stand of aspen there may be as many as 4,000 to 5,000 trees per acre. Many trees in Michigan can grow to be quite tall. White Pine trees may reach as high as 100 to 130 feet. At Hartwick State Park in Grayling there are trees that are estimated to be 150 feet tall or even taller.

Michigan's Healing Forests

One of the reasons that ancient man may have held the forests of Michigan in such awe is because there are many healing remedies in the woods. Native Americans used to boil white pine needles in water to make a tea that would prevent scurvy. White pine needles contain up to five times as much vitamin C as what is contained in an equal weight of lemons.

The Mohawk Indian name "Dirhon Dak" describes a group of Native Americans who were tree eaters. They ate quantities of the inner bark of trees and the tops of pines.

Primitive man had some very strange beliefs concerning various plants that can be found in Michigan. Some believed that garlic had the power to protect them from the evil eye and chase away evil. They believed that demons, witches, and vampires stayed away from this plant.

Some people used to say that evil spirits fled from the very smell of St. John's Wort. It is reported that some people used to wear this herb as an amulet to try to protect themselves from evil.

Michigan Mazes

During the middle ages many people built mazes in the courtyards of castles. Mazes and labyrinths are typically built by Europeans, however, there are a few mazes in Michigan.

There is a labyrinth constructed in the Dow Gardens in Midland, Michigan. The maze is constructed with long heaps of dirt set in various rows. On top of the various rows of dirt there are bushes, plants, and shrubs. The garden is interesting to visit. It has been there since the 1800's. There are terraced areas and old stairways, now overgrown with grass, moss and foliage.

There is a small stream flowing through the garden, and interesting pathways going all over the place. The grounds are similar to the grounds that were found in the courtyards of castles in the middle ages. If a person happens to be in the area, it is worthwhile to check it out.

Michigan's Hypnotic Animals

There are a few Michigan animals that appear to have hypnotic powers. There have been weasels that have been known to confuse their prey by doing a weird dance for them. Weasels have been seen running around in small circles leaping and dancing as they go. As they dance they keep getting closer and closer to their prey until they are close enough to eat them.

Some researchers think that weasels do this on purpose. Others think that weasels sometimes have intense irritation, such as parasitic worms in the brain. The weasel's movements are spastic.

Some people claim that snakes have hypnotic powers. An English missionary named William Ellis once described watching a snake hypnotize a mouse. Some researchers claim that when a snake fixes its gaze upon prey, the prey seems unable to move. However, this strange snake gaze may have something to do with the fact that snakes have no eyelids. There may be other Michigan animals that have hypnotic powers.

Water Riddles of Michigan

According to Muskegon resident and Michigan history teacher, Stan Woodward, there are water phenomenon in Michigan. Woodward claims that one summer in the early 1960's a group of teenagers were having a beach party at the Muskegon State Park. The weather is reported to have been normal, while the waves were calm. Woodward says that a band of teens around a campfire were suddenly soaked with water and seaweed, buried by a wave.

Woodward believes that the water and seaweed they were soaked with either fell from the sky or came from an inland tidal wave called a seiche. Tom Graf of the Land and Water Management Group in Lansing says that seiche activity does occur in Michigan. "There are seiches on the Great Lakes. They usually occur over Lake Erie. They are associated with high and low pressure centers. They usually occur when there is a strong front coming across the lake, where the water bodies are aligned with western winds.

If the wind is blowing in one direction consistently, the water level can drop dramatically at one end of the lake. There was at least one instance I know of where the water level rose 8 feet on one end of the lake over a six hour period."

Woodward also knows of another water phenomenon. This involves a river branch that flows in a different direction than all the other tributaries of the same river. This is the Winnepausaug branch of the Pere Marquette River. The native name of this branch means "northern current".

If you have an unusual
fact or phenomenon
about the great state of Michigan
or about an odd Michigander
and would like to see your story
in a future edition of
"*MYSTIC MICHIGAN*",
please send your information to:

Mark Jager
P.O. Box 24
Hersey, Michigan 49639

Explore the Phenomenal in Michigan's Nature – Discover the Bizarre in Michigan's Past with the
MYSTIC MICHIGAN SERIES

MYSTIC MICHIGAN PART 1-
Pictured Rocks – Floating Island –Largest Living Creature – Sanilac Petroglyphs – The Cadillac to Traverse City Indian Trail – The Legend of Lake Superior – Missaukee Mounds – Underwater Passages – The Ancient Forest – Michigan Pyramids – Michigan's Mystery Culture –Sea Monster – Bigfoot in Michigan – Treasure Troves – Mystery Canal – Michigan Mirage – Sinkholes – Michigan's Place on the Continent of Pangaea – Gravity Hill – Paulding Lights – Waterfalls – Caves – Ancient Volcanoes – Great Lakes Triangle – Strange Prehistoric Creatures – Meteorites – Michigan's Stonehenge – Ancient Michigan Tablets – Dolmen Altars – St. Elmo's Fire – Ghost Fire – Waterspouts – Green Sunsets – Raining Fish – Tornados of Fire – Water Running UP Hill – Ancient Geometrical Gardens – Spirit Island – Strange Shakings in Michigan – Michigan Dust Devils – Michigan Man Eaters – Sinking City – Ancient Statues – Weird Weather Patterns – Vikings in Michigan – The Village of Giants – Bottomless Lakes – The Island of Ill Repute – Ice Storms

MYSTIC MICHGAN PART 2-
Ancient Underwater Indian Trail – Mysterious Ancient Wall – Ancient Rivers of Fire – Michigan's Life Energy Scientist – Kitch-iti-kipi Michigan's Emerald Spring – Vanishing Stream – Mystery Stones – Floating Bridge – Bizarre Bird Attacks – Disappearing and reappearing Lake – Glowing Graves – Dinosaurs in Michigan – Living Headless Animal – Tallest People – Bizarre Deer encounters – Illusions of Gravity – Artesian Will City – Fantastic Ice Caves –Bridge of Stars – Hobos in Michigan – An Unusual Michigander – Above Ground Cemeteries – Ancient Circular Ruins – Invisible Mountain – Fireballs From the Skies – Ball Lightning – Disappearing Land Masses

MYSTIC MICHIGAN PART 3-
Gogamain, Michigan's Kingdom of Darkness – Strange Underwater Fish Sounds – Magical Singing Mouse – Passenger Pigeon – Earthquakes in Michigan – Michigan's Highest Point – Winter Wonderland Snow Secrets – Secret Weather Omens – Subconscious Designs – Strange Glowing Fungus – Cosmic Radio Station – Angel Encounter – Buried City - Faces in the Falls – Incredible Echo Chambers – Tree Tunnels – Invisible Walls – Ghost Towns – The Lake Michigan Blob- Nature Drums – Primitive Rock Paintings- Age Old Disc Factory – Ancient Observations – Mystic Earth Rings – Mysterious Missing Race – Enchanted Forest – Healing Forests – Mazes – Hypnotic Animals – Water Riddles

MYSTIC MICHIGAN PART 4-
Ruins of Rome – Mystic Tower – Mermaid – Michigan: Ancient Cemetery – 1999 Fireball Phenomenon – Subterranean World – Hemlock Lights – Treasure Island Hermit – Strange Animal Encounters – Lake Erie's Fairy Grotto – Underwater Forest – Michigan's Circle and Square – Lights of Denton Road – Reappearing Historic Ship – Forest Cemeteries – Lost Gold Mine – Underwater Metropolis – Medieval Michigan – Explosion Oddity – Strange Earth Design – Strange Rivers – Underwater Roads – Will-o-wisp – House of David – Rock Face – Island Treasure – Geometric Formations – Ancient Underwater Structure – Meteorite Islands

MYSTIC MICHIGAN PART 5-
Walled Lake – Phantom Train – Oakwood Cemetery Gravity Hill – Phantom Ships – Norway Forest Light – Mystic Stream – The Portage Lake Story – Buried Prehistoric Beast – Bellevue Ruins – Balloon Bombs in Michigan – Haserot Beach Mystery – Unusual Boulder – Huge Ancient Cataclysm – Mysterious Garden Island – Stannard Rock – Strange Grand Rapids Mound – Ancient 1,000 Acre Garden – Disappearing House – Strange Lake Craters – Ancient Stairway – Michigan's Biggest Trees – Mystery Sphere – Labyrinth – Ancient 2 Acre Horseshoe – Underwater Casino – Acid Lake – Shoe Tree – An Amazing Canyon – Michigan's Scandinavian Landscape

MYSTIC MICHIGAN PART 6-
Crop Circles - More Michigan Mastodons - Whispering Waters – Whirlpools - Stationary Whirlwind - Great Lake Sharks - Flying Campfires - Ancient Parking Lots - Iargo Springs - Strange Animal Screams - Underground Factory - Ancient Cemetery Island - Mystic Lights of Paris - Durant's Castle - Meteorite Fires - Hexen Rings - Singing Sands - Michigan's Giant Gem - Underwater Sinkholes - Underwater Mountains - Ancient Buried Forest - Great Lakes Catastrophe - Ancient Underwater Woodland - Natural underwater Monument - Underwater Maze - Michigan's Earthwork Alignments - Michigan Mimetoliths - Ancient River Beds

MYSTIC MICHIGAN PART 7-
Ancient War Mine - The Bottle House - Stone Chambers - Pre- Glacial - Turnip Rock - Eerie Pere Cheney - The Legend of Silver Mountain - Magnetic Abnormality - The Michigan/Wizard of Oz Connection - Ancient Explosion - King Solomon's Mines? - Michigan's Brigadoon - Huge Statues - Echo Canyons - Wilderness Column of Water - Michigan's New Stonehenge - Amazing Dunes - Arrowhead Finds - The Orbs of Nunica Cemetery - Ancient Library of Rock - A Very Large Piece of Copper - Phenomenal Painting - Michigan's Lost Peninsula - Michigan's Continental Divide - The Mystic Rainbow - The River That Flows Both Ways

MYSTIC MICHGANDER
MYSTIC MICHIGAN PART 1 AUDIOBOOK
TRIPPING AMERICA THE FANTASTIC

ORDER FORM

The following items are available by
Mark Jager

Qty.	Item	Total
	Mystic Michigan #1... $7.95	
	Mystic Michigan #2... $7.95	
	Mystic Michigan #3... $7.95	
	Mystic Michigan #4... $7.95	
	Mystic Michigan #5... $7.95	
	Mystic Michigan #6... $7.95	
	Mystic Michigan #7... $7.95	
	Mystic Michigander... $7.95	
	Mystic Michigan #1 Audio Book ... $12.95	
	Tripping America The Fantastic ... $7.95	
	SUBTOTAL	
	SHIPPING	
	TOTAL	

SHIPPING CHARGES

Please send $3.50 for shipping & handling for the first item purchased. Add $0.25 for each additional item.

THANK YOU!

Name_____

Street_____

City_____State_____Zip_____

Send order with check or money order to:

Mark Jager
PO Box 24
Hersey, MI 49639

Orders ship USPS
Allow 1 week for delivery

Notes

Notes